GW00363291

To..........

From....................

Purple Ronnie's
Little Book for
The World's Best
D ✪ A ✪ D

by Purple Ronnie

First published 2009 by Boxtree
an imprint of Pan Macmillan Ltd
Pan Macmillan, 20 New Wharf Road, London N1 9RR
Basingstoke and Oxford
Associated companies throughout the world
www.panmacmillan.com

ISBN 978-0-7522-2699-6

Copyright © Purple Enterprises Ltd, a Coolabi company 2009

All rights reserved. No part of this publication may be
reproduced, stored in or introduced into a retrieval system, or
transmitted, in any form, or by any means (electronic, mechanical,
photocopying, recording or otherwise) without the prior written
permission of the publisher. Any person who does any unauthorized
act in relation to this publication may be liable to criminal
prosecution and civil claims for damages.

9 8 7 6 5 4 3 2 1

A CIP catalogue record for this book is
available from the British Library.

Printed and bound in Hong Kong

'Purple Ronnie' created by Giles Andreae. The right of Giles Andreae and Janet Cronin
to be identified respectively as the author and illustrator of this work has been asserted by them
in accordance with the Copyright, Designs and Patents Act 1988.

Visit www.panmacmillan.com to read more about all our books
and to buy them. You will also find features, author interviews and
news of any author events, and you can sign up for e-newsletters
so that you're always first to hear about our new releases.

dazzle

shine

a poem for a

Star Dad

Has anyone recently told
you

How totally smashing you
are

If not here's a message
to tell you

That this person thinks
you're a star

Remember

Dads are hardly ever at their best first thing in the morning

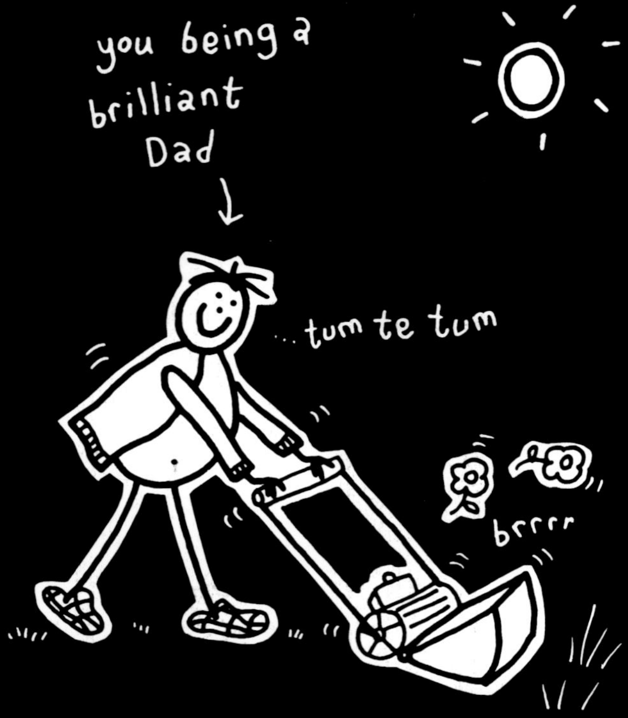
you being a brilliant Dad
...tum te tum
brrrr

a poem for ↓

My Smashing Dad

Your tummy's spreading
out a bit
Your hair is getting thinner
But none of that's
important

Cos I say you're a
winner!

Dads and Gadgets

Dads can hardly ever resist a really good new gadget

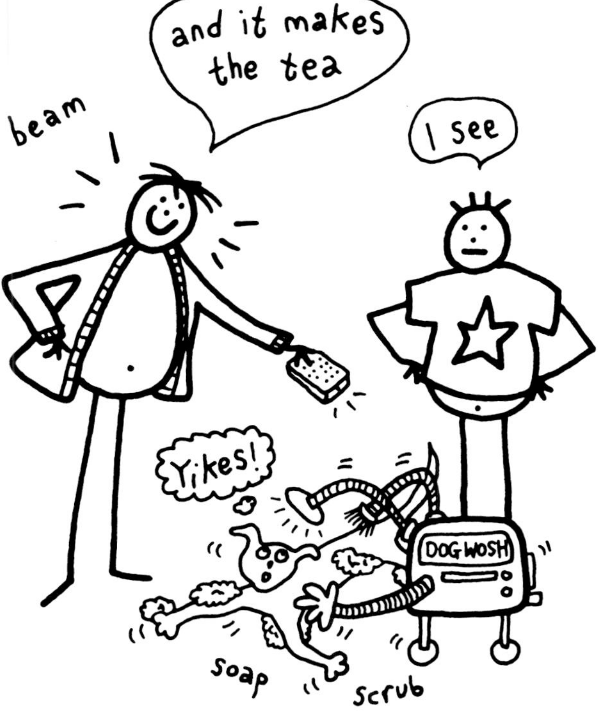
beam
and it makes the tea
I see
Yikes!
DOG WOSH
soap
scrub

a poem about

Lazy Dads

Some Dads do the cleaning

While Mums go off to work

But some just turn the
telly on

Then crack a beer and
shirk!

Warning :—

As Dads get older
they start growing
hair in the weirdest
places

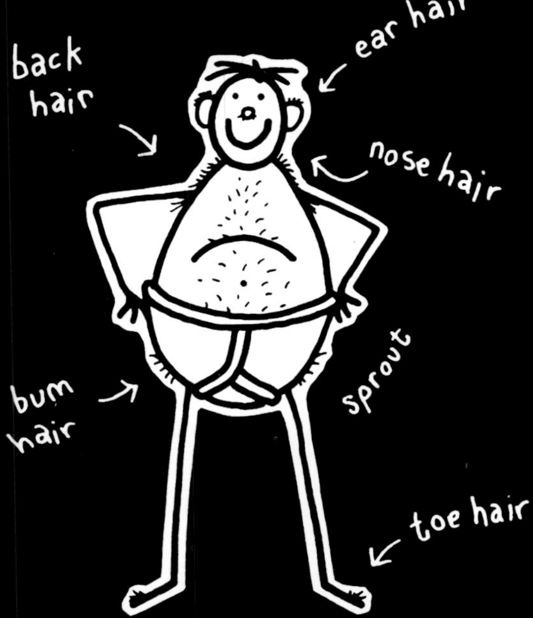
back hair
ear hair
nose hair
sprout
bum hair
toe hair

a poem about

My Dad and Footie

My dad is mostly quiet

He's really not a lout

But when he's watching
                footie

You ought to hear him
                shout !

Competitive Dads

Some Dads always
want to be the best
at everything

a poem for

My Fab Dad

Sometimes as Dads become older
Their hair starts to vanish away
Their tummies go saggy
Their bottoms go baggy
But you just get better each day

Special Tip

Even Dads need hugs

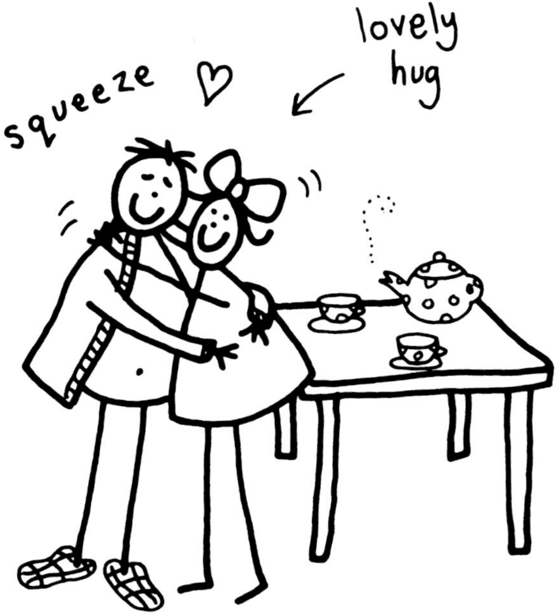

squeeze
lovely hug

a poem about

Dads

Some dads think if they
took charge

That life would be a ball

But somehow mums and
children

Seem to always spoil it all !

Smooth Dads

Beware — What your Dad thinks is smooth is hardly ever the same as what your friends think is smooth

oh yes, I was a bit of a ladies man - cocktail, Señorita?
umm...
cringe
strain
horrid red trousers

a poem about my
Groovy Dad

Sometimes people's fathers
Can be boring, dull or rude.
But my Dad is fantastic
Cos he's such a groovy
dude

Fact :-

All Dads are really just little boys at heart

coming through!
woo! woo!
you can have a go in a minute
it's my train set

Dad's Boasting

Thanks for thinking well
of me
And thanks for being proud

But, Dad, when we're in
company

Please don't boast so loud!

oh yes, straight As in everything... absolute genius... always knew it blah blah
cringe
beam
v. sexy rock star

Some Dads just can't accept that they're not as young as they used to be

a poem about

Dads and Driving

With Dad to teach me
driving
I'm sure I just can't fail
But why's he looking wobbly
And why's he turned so
pale?

Sporty Dads

The great thing about Sporty Dads is you always know what to get them for their birthday

My Lovely Dad

Some Dads play golf at
the weekend

Or sail in their boats out
at sea

But others just love to
laze out in a chair

And watch loads of sport
on TV

Interesting Point

Although Mums
hardly ever fart,
Dads hardly ever stop

a poem for ↓

My Dad

This poem is specially to
tell you

The reason why you are so
great

You're not only brilliant at
being my Dad

You're also a really top
mate

Warning:-

Dads can be the most embarrassing dancers ever

a poem about

Dad's Jokes

My face has gone all red
and hot

My toes are tightly curled

Cos my dad's silly jokes
must be

The worst ones in the world!

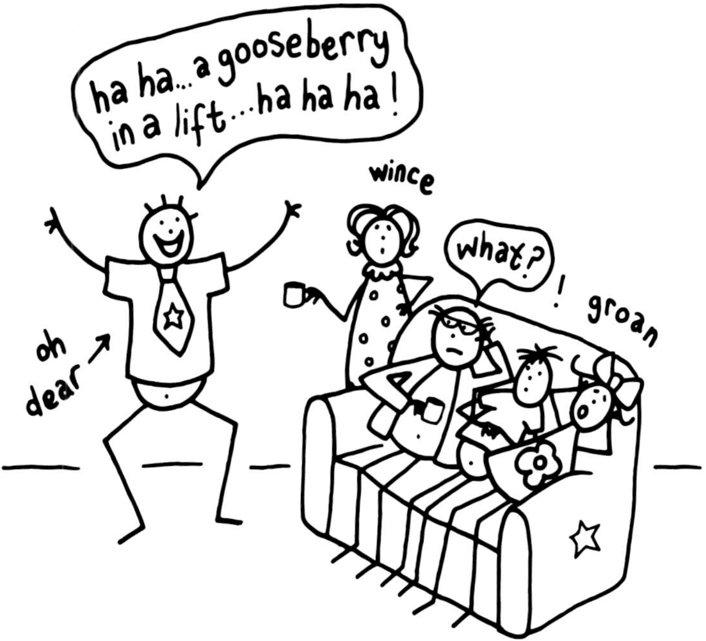
ha ha... a gooseberry in a lift...ha ha ha!
wince
what?
!
groan
oh dear

Dads and the Lav

Most Dads love
nothing more than
a really good session
on the lav

My Dad's Lectures

My Dad loves to lecture
And waffle like a prof
I wish there was a button
So that I could turn him
off!

Special Tip

From time to time
Dads love to be
told they're a hero

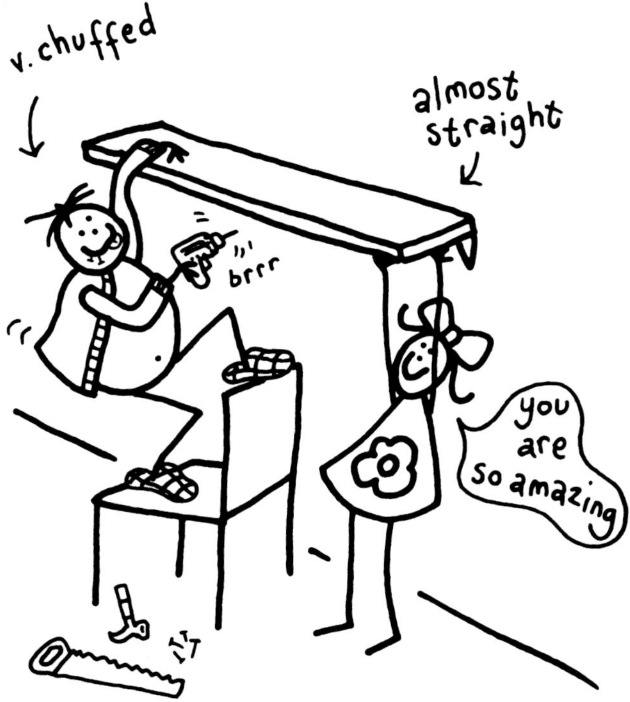
v. chuffed
almost straight
brrr
you are so amazing

a poem for
↓
My Perfect Dad

Some fathers can be
boring

And some can be quite
mad

But I am really lucky

Cos you're the p<u>erfect</u>
Dad!

Dad's Garden

Our Dad loves his garden

It's full of fruits and
flowers

I wonder why he stays
out there

For hours and hours and hours...?

Sometimes you can forget just how useful Dads really are